AMBER LEA

Phoenix Travel and Restaurant Guide

Guide to Discovering Phoenix Area Attractions, Restaurants and More for the Tourist and Weekend Getaways

First edition

This book was professionally typeset on Reedsy.
Find out more at reedsy.com

Contents

1

Welcome!

Let me be the first one to welcome you to the Phoenix, Arizona area. I am excited you have chosen this pocket size guide to assist with your trip, whether traveling as a couple, with your family, flying solo or whether you are a local and are looking to see what else the Phoenix area has to offer. This guide is designed to provide each traveler with several handfuls of information and tips to consider and help with planning their trip to this wonderful, beautiful diamond in the rough. Desert, as it may be, Arizona has a lot to offer.

To provide a little background about myself...I traveled here for the first time in the late 90s and immediately fell in love. It was then that I decided to relocate to the Phoenix area. So whether you visit for a girls' trip, a golf tournament, your honeymoon, anniversary, family reunion, or want to see and experience something different without leaving the country....come on over. Something that I learned during my visit was we get all four seasons, including much snow in the northern part of the state. If you come in the winter, you can go skiing two to three hours north of Phoenix...then drive down to the Phoenix area and not even need a jacket. So yes, the terrain changes quite a bit the further north you drive...from desert Saguaro cactus and mesquite to beautiful tall pine trees in the northern forests.

Not only is Arizona known for one of the Wonders of the World, the Grand Canyon, the Phoenix/ Scottsdale area is also home to some of the best spas and golf courses.

You might want to bring your passport as we are about four hours from a famous tourist beach area, Rocky Point, Mexico. There are plenty of inexpensive vacation homes and places to stay in Rocky Point. Very nice restaurants as well.

This guide will give you some highlights and plenty of information but not every detail about Phoenix. When you are wondering what you can do on a particular day, would like to take a day trip, or would like to get a bite to eat, then you can reference your trusty guide here. There is plenty here at your fingertips to save you from having to spend crazy time online figuring out an area that is new to you or that may have changed the last time you visited. Please look at this as a condensed reference guide to help you maximize your time and see some of your options you may not have known were available.

Please enjoy your visit and be sure to bring a camera as you will surely have many, many moments you would like to look back on when you return home, share with others and reminisce about.

2

Planning Your Trip

You will likely fly in to Phoenix Sky Harbor International Airport (PHX). The airport is fairly easy to navigate. There are 3 terminals with the major airlines. When you arrive at PHX, you will be located just south of downtown Phoenix. There are shuttles to the rental car depot and area hotels. There is also a lite rail that you can catch at the end of the airport SkyTrain.

Rental Car / Transportation

The rental car depot is located a few minutes from the airport and houses all of the rental car companies. Here is where you will pick up and drop off your rental car. There is a shuttle that will also take you back to the airport for your return home flight.

There are lite rails that run through downtown Phoenix and several other major areas. There are city buses that also run. Depending on your preference, there is Uber or Lyft. And if you are planning to pretty much stay in the downtown area, there are scooter and bike rental stations. You also have the option to rent a car for a few hours or for the day with ZipCar.

Where to Stay

There are several options for your stay while here in the Phoenix area. All of the major name hotels are in the area as well as a healthy amount of AirBnB options. Arizona is also a major area for timeshares.

To name just a few sites to price hotels with:

- Expedia
- Priceline
- Travelocity
- Tripadvisor

Weather Year-round (averages in Fahrenheit)

January 68/45
February 72/48
March 77/52
April 86/59
May 94/67
June 104/76
July 106/82
August 105/81
September 100/75
October 89/64
November 76/51
December 68/44

Please be aware and careful of the temperatures in the summer. They are capable of rising above the temperature averages stated above. Take extra precautions (extra water, stay cool, and wear sunscreen.)

Supermarkets

There are several supermarket options in the area. To help you to know what to look for, here is a list of our supermarkets, some of which you may very well be familiar with:

- Safeway
- Fry's Marketplace
- Basha's
- Sprouts Farmers Markets
- Whole Foods
- Trader Joe's
- WinCo Foods
- AJ's Fine Foods
- Food City Supermarket
- El Super
- Lee Lee International Supermarket (Asian grocery store)
- U-Bate African and Caribbean Store

Pharmacy

The pharmacies chains or stores with pharmacies are located in Arizona:

- Walgreens
- CVS
- Walmart
- Most of the supermarkets also have a pharmacy.

3

Arizona Summers vs Arizona Winters

A known fact about Arizona is the warmth of the summers. To protect yourself and those who may be traveling with you, please be sure to bring the following with you or purchase them soon upon your arriving:

- Make sure you have access to A/C where you are staying and, in your car
- Drink plenty of water / electrolyte drinks (like Gatorade)
- Wear loose fitted clothes (light colors)
- Swim
- Stay in cool places
- Carry water in car (disposable cooler, kept out of direct sunlight)
- Avoid sitting in the car for any extended amount of time
- Wear sun protection (sunscreen, hat, sunglasses)
- Become familiar with signs of heat stroke or heat exhaustion
- An umbrella can do wonders as well as most shaded areas

4

Top Attractions

To the surprise of many, the Phoenix area has quite a variety of activities to suit everyone.... Whether you are looking for something to do outdoors or looking for a nice, cool air conditioned activity, you will find several different things to enjoy.

Desert Botanical Gardens
1201 N. Galvin Pkwy
Phoenix, AZ 85008

Phoenix Zoo
455 N. Galvin Pkwy
Phoenix, AZ 85008

Odysea Aquarium
9500 E. Via de Ventura, A100
Scottsdale, AZ 85256
Laser & Mirror Maze
Featured at Odysea. An experience for the mind with mazes and mirrors providing infinite reflections.

Butterfly Wonderland
9500 E. Via de Ventura, F100
Scottsdale, AZ 85256

Musical Instrument Museum
4725 E. Mayo Blvd
Phoenix, AZ 85050

Arizona Science Center
600 E. Washington St.
Phoenix, AZ 85004

Civic Space Park
424 N. Central Ave.
Phoenix, AZ 85004

Hall of Flame Fire Museum
6101 E. Van Buren St.
Phoenix, AZ 85008

Arizona Museum of Natural History (Dino Museum)
53 N. MacDonald
Mesa, AZ 85201

Legoland Discovery Center Arizona
5000 S. Arizona Mills Cir.
Tempe, AZ 85282

Castles 'n Coasters
9445 N. Metro Pkwy E.
Phoenix, AZ 85051

Sea Life Aquarium
5000 S. Arizona Mills Cir.
Tempe, AZ 85282

Tovrea Castle at Carraro Heights
5025 E. Van Buren St.
Phoenix, AZ 85008

Oasis Water Park
8000 Arizona Grand Pkwy
Phoenix, AZ 85044

Japanese Friendship Garden
1125 N. 3rd Ave.
Phoenix, AZ 85003

You can take a nice peaceful, quiet stroll through this beautiful garden (3.5 acres) in downtown Phoenix, which includes a tea house and tea garden.

Art District
333 E. Roosevelt St.
Phoenix, AZ 85004

The first Friday of each month, the Art District comes alive. Artists welcome visitors. It is one of the country's largest self-guided art walks. And it happens in Downtown Phoenix. Come on by and look around at what artists in the area have to offer. Along Roosevelt Row, you will be entertained by music, pop-up markets and even food trucks.

Scottsdale Museum of Contemporary Art
7374 E. 2nd St.
Scottsdale, AZ 85251

Scottsdale Museum of Contemporary Art

Arcosanti (1:20 North of Phoenix)
13555 S. Cross L Road
Mayer, AZ 86333
Arcosanti is a place of ongoing architecture experiments, art, ecology and community. You can take tours and see demonstrations, shop, explore, hike, stay overnight and more.

Fiesta Bowl Museum
7135 E. Camelback Rd.
Scottsdale, AZ 85251
This museum features college football memorabilia and all the subdivision helmets, all 120 of them.

Goldfield Ghost Town and Mine Tours
4650 N. Mammoth Mine Rd.
Apache Junction, AZ 85119
This awesome town is located about 45 minutes east of Phoenix. When you arrive, you feel like you have stepped back in time. Looks like an old western town. There is a new feature. They now have a ZIPLINE. There are tours, a railroad, shopping, entertainment, horseback riding, a saloon and more.

Out of Africa
3505 AZ-260
Camp Verde, AZ 86322
Arizona's very own wildlife zoo featuring animals like lions, slots, lemurs, tigers, giraffes, and many, many more. Way too many to list.

Bearizona Wildlife Park

1500 E. Rt. 66
Williams, AZ 86046

Bearizona is a drive-thru, up close and personal experience of several different animals. Keep your doors and windows closed. Yes, this is a self-guided tour through the wilderness.

Arizona Distilling Company
601 W. University Ave.
Tempe, AZ 85281

Huss Uptown Phoenix Taproom + Kitchen
100 E. Camelback Rd.
Phoenix, AZ 85281

Cactus TapRoom
20429 N. Lake Pleasant Rd.
Peoria, AZ 85382

Arizona Wine Tours Blasian
2323 E. Magnolia St.
Phoenix, AZ 85034

Desert Rock Winery and Distillery
7302 E. Helm Dr.
Scottsdale, AZ 85260

Taliesin West
12621 N. Frank Lloyd Wright Blvd
Scottsdale, AZ 85259

Frank Lloyd Wright's winter home and studio until he passed away. Now it is the headquarters of his foundation and is open to the public for tours.

Grand Canyon

Pictures do not do this Wonder of the World justice. You must experience the Grand Canyon in person. There are a few ways to get there. You could drive and enjoy the scenery and hit a few key areas along the way like Prescott, Sedona, Flagstaff and Jerome. There is also the option to sit back and enjoy the scenic view from the train that departs from Williams, Arizona. You could opt to do a turnaround trip in a day or stay overnight. There are also buses from Phoenix. You also have the option to fly from Sky Harbor Airport (PHX) to Flagstaff (FLG).

Sedona

The home of the red rocks. There is so much here to explore. Like the Grand Canyon, you must experience Sedona in person. You have the nicely marked scenic drive that lets you know where most of the scenic spots and lookouts are for nice walks and photo opportunities. Then there are the jeep tours if you want to get off the usual path and get down and dirty and set aside the hiking while still getting some nice exploring in with a guide with Pink Adventure Tours or one of the other jeep or ATV tour companies. There are tons of shopping and restaurants in Sedona. One of the main areas to shop in the heart of town is Tlaquepaque Arts and Shopping Village. Sedona also has mountain biking trails. A list of trails and information are listed below.

Old Town Scottsdale

Old Town Scottsdale is a tourist favorite one town over from Phoenix. You will find plenty of shopping, restaurants, spas, galleries, and more. It is an entire neighborhood that runs from Fashion Square Mall several blocks south of Indian School Road. A concentrated section of shops begin south of Indian School Road at Scottsdale Road.

Cave Creek

This Wild West town is just north of Phoenix and has plenty to do and several places to eat.

Cave Creek Museum
6140 E. Skyline Dr.
Cave Creek, AZ 85331

Cave Creek Cave

The Cave of Cave Creek is about 1 ½ miles from the heart of Cave Creek

Frontier Town

6245 E. Cave Creek Rd
Cave Creek, AZ 85331

Carefree Desert Gardens

101 Easy St.
Carefree, AZ 85377

Wild at Heart

31840 N. 45th St.
Cave Creek, AZ 85331

Wild at Heart rehabilitates, rescues and releases birds of prey here in Arizona. There are limited tours from April to August.

Rare Earth Gallery

6401 E. Cave Creek Rd.
Cave Creek, AZ 85331

Awesome place to visit and shop. This is the largest home decor store that is filled with items that are natural earth items. Rare Earth offers a multitude of items made from crystals, fossils, minerals, and more. Many that stand several feet tall. From decor to jewelry to keepsakes.

The Boulders Resort and Spa

34631 N. Tom Darlington Dr.
Scottsdale, AZ 85262
(480) 488-9009

Carefree Farmers Market
101 Easy Street
Town of Carefree Sundial
Carefree, AZ 85377

Carefree Sundial
Sundial Circle and E. Carefree Dr.
Town of Carefree Sundial
Carefree, AZ 85377

Spur Cross Ranch Conservation
44000 N. Spur Cross Rd.
Cave Creek, AZ 85331

Canyons / National Parks / Lakes

Antelope Canyon
Page, AZ

This canyon, which is one of the most popular and most photographed canyons, is a little over 4 hours north of Phoenix in Page Arizona. There are two sections to this canyon. Upper Antelope Canyon called "The Crack" and Lower Antelope Canyon called "The Corkscrew".

Canyon de Chelly

You can catch free guided hikes each weekend in the summer at the Visitor's Center for Canyon de Chelly. This beautiful site is definitely a national monument and is found on a Navajo reservation in Eastern Arizona. You will also have the pleasure of seeing Native American ruins and Spider Rock.

An Insider's Guide to the Four Corners · National Parks Conservation Association can be found on their website.

Canyon Lake

This lake has unusual rock formations and hidden coves and visitor favorite – Dolly Steamboat. This lake is perfect for picnics, sightseeing, water skiing, fishing, etc. Located in the Superstition Mountains.

Lake Pleasant

Lake Pleasant Regional

Located on the northwest border of Phoenix within the municipal boundaries of Peoria.

This is a major recreational hub for this area of Phoenix.

Tempe Town Lake

550 E. Tempe Town Lake

Mill Ave and Rio Salado Pkwy

Tempe, AZ 85281

This lake is located closer to Phoenix. You have the option to rent pedal boats, bikes, donut boats and more.

Saguaro Lake

Tonto National Forest

Mesa, AZ

This lake offers fishing, boating and water sports.

Horseshoe Lake

A quiet, remote lake great for relaxing and recreation. Located in Tonto National Forest.

* Please reference park sites to ensure whether there are entrance fees or not.

5

Shopping

There is quite a few shopping oasis here to choose from. Each one has its own flavor. You can still find many of your usual favorites, but you see many that are unique to the area.

Phoenix Shopping

Biltmore Fashion Park
2502 E. Camelback Rd.
Phoenix, AZ 85016

Tanger Outlet
6800 N. 95th Ave.
Glendale, AZ 85305

Desert Ridge Marketplace
21001 N. Tatum Blvd
Phoenix, AZ 85050

Phoenix Premium Outlets

4976 Premium Outlet way
Chandler, AZ 85226

Tempe Marketplace
2000 E. Rio Salado Pkwy
Tempe, AZ 85281

Arrowhead Towne Center
Northwest side of Phoenix
7700 W. Arrowhead Towne Center
Glendale, AZ 85308

The Shops at Norterra
North Phoenix
2450 W. Happy Valley Rd.
Phoenix, AZ 85085

Uptown Plaza
100 E. Camelback Rd.
Phoenix, AZ 85012

Park Central Shopping Mall (Encanto Village)
3121 N. 3rd Ave.
Phoenix, AZ 85013
This strip mall is located on Central Avenue and Osborn Road

Scottsdale Shopping

Scottsdale Fashion Square
7014 E. Camelback Rd.
Scottsdale, AZ 85251

Hilton Village
6015-6155 N. Scottsdale Rd.
Scottsdale, AZ 85250

The Shops Gainey Village
8777 N. Scottsdale Rd.
Scottsdale, AZ 85253
Old Town Scottsdale
Scottsdale Rd and Indian School Rd

Scottsdale Pavilions
9120 E. Talking Stick Way (FKA - Indian Bend Rd.)
Salt River Pima - Indian Community
Scottsdale, AZ 85250

El Pedregal Festival Marketplace
34505 N. Scottsdale Rd.
Scottsdale, AZ 85266
(480) 488-2190

Kierland Commons
15205 N. Kierland Blvd
Scottsdale, AZ 85254

Scottsdale Waterfront
7135 E. Camelback Rd
Scottsdale, AZ 85251

5th Avenue Shops of Scottsdale
Original Arts and Crafts area in Scottsdale
E. 5th Ave.

Scottsdale, AZ 85251

Scottsdale Quarter
15279 N. Scottsdale Rd.
Scottsdale, AZ 85254

6

Golf Courses

Golfing is a very common part of life here. Golf courses here are very easy to come by. By all means, bring your clubs with you and enjoy yourself out on the green.

Cave Creek Golf Course
15202 N. 19th Ave.
Phoenix, AZ
(602) 534-GOLF

Lookout Mountain Golf Club
11111 N. 7th St (In Hilton Phoenix Tapatio Cliffs Resort)
Phoenix, AZ 85020
(602) 866-6357

Palo Verde Golf Course
6215 N. 15th Ave.
Phoenix, AZ
(602) 534-GOLF

Wildfire Golf Club
5350 E. Marriott Dr. (In JW Marriott Phoenix)
Phoenix, AZ
(602) 534-GOLF

Grand Canyon University Golf Course
5902 W. Indian School Rd.
Phoenix, AZ 85033
(623) 846-4022

Stonecreek Golf Club
4435 E. Paradise Village Pkwy S.
Phoenix, AZ 85032
(602) 953-9111

7

Spas / Massages

The Phoenix / Scottsdale area is also known for its spas. You can find some of the most prestigious spas here. You can spend a day getting pampered at the spa or get refreshed with the massage of your choice.

Sanctuary Camelback Resort's Spa
5700 E. McDonald Dr.
Paradise Valley, AZ 85018
(855) 680-3239

Healing Harbor Spa - Scottsdale
11000 N. Scottsdale Rd.
Suite 160
Scottsdale, AZ 85254
(480) 999-6200

Mary Lynn's Massage and Day Spa
7297 N. Scottsdale Rd.
Unit 1004
Paradise Valley, AZ 85253
(480) 859-7777

Arizona Grand Resort & Spa
8000 Arizona Grand Pkwy
Phoenix, AZ 85044
(877) 800-4888

Massage Escapes
1855 W. Greenway Rd.
Phoenix, AZ 85023
(602) 547-2639

Elements Massage
630 E. Bell Rd.
Phoenix, AZ 85022
(480) 648-1238

Serenity Massage
7650 S. McClintock Dr.
Suite 111
Tempe, AZ 85284
(480) 755-2323

Massage Envy
Several locations in the Phoenix area.

Hawaiian Experience Spa
11300 E. Via Linda
Ste E
Scottsdale, AZ 85259
(480) 661-2991

New Serenity Spa
15609 N. Hayden Rd
Scottsdale, AZ 85260
(480) 998-6991

Authentic Thai Massage
7159 E. Main St.
Old Town Scottsdale, AZ 85251
(602) 606-7707

Mens Spa
4375 N. 75th St.
Ste B
Scottsdale, AZ 85251
(480) 686-8538
A spa just for men. They can have their day at the spa too and be

pampered.

Movement Restoration

6747 E. Thomas Rd.

Suite 104

Scottsdale, AZ 85251

(480) 612-5090

Movement Restoration uses their massage therapy to focus restoring natural body movement through individual massage treatments working to improve and increase circulation, flexibility and range of motion.

Castle Hot Springs Resort

5050 N. Castle Hot Springs Rd.

Morristown, AZ 85342

This resort is one hour outside of Phoenix. Experience the hot springs, guided e-bike tours, wellness classes, horseback riding, archery, utv tours, and much more.

8

Hot Air Balloon Rides

A beautiful attraction is to take a hot air balloon ride over the Arizona desert. Here are a few ways to book your excursion.

APEX Hot Air Balloon Rides

(877) 946-8247

Rainbow Ryders Hot Air Balloon Company
(480)299-0154

Arizona Balloon Safaris
(480) 502-7640
Super extra large riding basket and you can have breakfast during the sunrise ride.

Destination Balloon Rides
(302) 236-7425

9

Horseback Riding

It is not unusual to see a cowgirl or cowboy riding through parts of town. You are more than welcome to take a leisurely horse ride and enjoy another part of the wild wild west.

Trailhead Ranch
35013 N. 49th St.
Cave Creek, AZ 85331
(480) 488-2251

Trailhead offers rides along scenic trails in the beautiful Foothills desert.

Wild West Trail Rides
48606 N. 17th Ave.
New River, AZ 85087
(602) 316-3360

Wild West Trail Rides is open from November to April. Kohls Ranch Stables is open from May to October.

MacDonald's Ranch
26540 N. Scottsdale Rd.
Scottsdale, AZ 85255

MacDonald's Ranch has a variety of activities besides horseback riding. They have a petting zoo, cowboy cookouts, panning for gold, a hay-bale maze, lawn games and plenty of photo ops.

10

Best Hiking

Be sure to prepare ahead of time for your hikes. Good, supportive walking shoes are very important. The sun can be intense depending on the time of year you are heading out. So always protect your skin – breathable clothing, sunscreen, hat, cooling cloth, etc. Cannot stress enough that having plenty of water is essential. Especially if you are taking a longer hike, perhaps carry a backpack with a few essentials (water, small first aid kit, phone, flare, walking stick, compass, snacks, map, multi-utility tool, flashlight, matches, sunglasses, change of clothing).

Camelback Mountain via Echo Canyon Trail

Echo Canyon Recreation Area, Phoenix, AZ

2.5 miles (Hard)

This is one of Phoenix's best spots for hiking and rock climbing and offers great views over the Phoenix / Scottsdale metropolitan area. Very popular.

Hole In the Rock

625 N. Galvin Pkwy

Phoenix, AZ 85008

0.3 miles (Easy)

There is a gem at the end of this hike. A short hike to a unique spot to see the Phoenix skyline.

North Mountain

North Mountain Park

10608 N 7th St.

Phoenix, AZ 85020

1.7 miles (Moderate)

This trail offers excellent views of North Phoenix and Downtown Phoenix. The trail surface is asphalt and dirt and is and is an out and back trail. You get a good cardio workout as the trail is steep.

Circumference Trail to Ridgeline Trail Loop

Deems Hills Recreation Area

Phoenix, AZ 85083

3.8 miles (Moderate)

Along with commanding awesome views, this trail loop traverses the Deems Hills Recreation Area.

Piestewa Peak Summit Trail

Phoenix Mountain Preserve

2701 E. Squaw Peak Dr.

Phoenix, AZ 85016

2.1 miles (Hard)

This trail is a hidden gem. This trail is tucked away off of Route 51 and Glendale Avenue. Along with the trails, there are nice, covered picnic areas.

Pyramid Trail

South Mountain Preserve

South Mountain Park and Preserve

10919 S. Central Ave.

Phoenix, AZ 85042

6.0 miles (Moderate)

South Mountain Park is the largest municipal park in the United States. And one of the largest urban parks in the world.

Lookout Mountain Summit Trail

Phoenix Mountain Preserve

14441 N 18th St.

Phoenix, AZ 85022

0.9 miles (Moderate)

The trail is near Paradise Valley in the Phoenix Mountain Preserve.

Pinnacle Peak Trail

Pinnacle Peak Park

26802 N 102nd Way

Scottsdale, AZ 85262

4.0 miles (Moderate)

Sunrise Peak via Sunrise Trail

McDowell Sonoran Preserve

Scottsdale, AZ 85259

4.3 miles (Moderate)

Treasure Loop Trail

Tonto National Forest

Apache Junction, AZ 85119

2.3 miles (Moderate)

This beautiful trail has unique rock formations and beautiful wildflowers.

Devil's Bridge Trail
Coconino National Forest
Sedona, AZ
3.9 miles (Moderate)

Cathedral Rock Trail
Coconino National Forest
Sedona, AZ
1.2 miles (Hard)

Coconino National Forest is one of the most breathtaking and unforgettable areas in the country – Sedona, Arizona. Beautiful red rock formations. Sedona is 2 hours north of Phoenix.

Teacup Trail to Coffeepot Rock
2050 Buena Vista Dr.
Coconino National Forest
Sedona, AZ
2.7 miles (Easy)

This is a good trail for family hikes and walking the dog and features stunning red rock views.

Horseshoe Bend Trail
Glen Canyon National Recreation Area
1.5 miles (Easy)

This beautiful hike is located in the Paria Canyon-Vermillion Cliffs Wilderness Area is a little over 4 hours north of Phoenix, east of the Grand Canyon.

11

Best Mountain Biking Trails

Decide you would like to bike the trails today instead of hiking, we have you covered. You can rent the mountain of your choice. Then hit some beautiful trails laid out throughout the area.

Phoenix

Exhale Bikes
2814 W. Bell Rd.
Phoenix, AZ 85053

Landis Cyclery
4 locations throughout the Phoenix, Scottsdale and Tempe

Best Trails (Phoenix area)

- Black Canyon Trail
- South Mountain Park
- McDowell Mountain Park
- Desert Classic
- Sonoran Preserve North

These and many more trails can be found on the mtbproject website.

Sedona

Thunder Mountain Bikes
1695 W. State Rt. 89A
Sedona, AZ 86336

Best Trails (Sedona area)

- Aerie Cockscomb Loop Trail
- Mescal Trail
- Chuckwagon Trail
- Llama Trail

- Long Canyon Trail to Deadman's Flat Trail

This is just to name a few trails in the Sedona area. Additional trails can be found on the PlanetWare website.

12

Hidden Gems - Activities

As if the other activities were not enough, here are a few you may not have been aware of. You will definitely want to get your camera ready and make sure you have plenty of memory.

Phoenix Bat Caves

3698-3694 E. Colter St.

Phoenix, AZ 85018

Every night at dusk, this man-made cement tunnel structure became home to bats who put on a show every night at dusk. They sleep through the day then come out at night to eat the usual mosquitoes and bugs.

Mystery Castle

800 E. Mineral Rd.

Phoenix, AZ 85042

This gem is open from October through May. Very eccentric and innovative sight. This 18-room castle is made of stone, adobe, car parts, salvaged rail tracks, telephone poles among other things. You will be surprised what makes up this castle.

Wigwam Village
811 W. Hopi Dr.
Holbrook, AZ 86025
Here you have hotel suites made up of wigwams. Nicely priced as well.

Curious Nature
5032 N. Central Ave.
Phoenix, AZ 85012
This gem is located Downtown Phoenix. Labeled a fine science and natural history emporium, Curious Nature has everything from taxidermy, bones, skulls, exotic plants, collectible items and gifts. They have museum quality specimens and an assortment of oddities that are ever-changing.

Arizona Falls
5802 E. Indian School Rd.
Phoenix, AZ 85018
Originally built in 1902 to bring power to the city, this spot now serves as a local and tourist gem. Come relax and take in some history about our Falls and have a picnic at the same time.

Circle 6 Studios
1424 E. Virginia Ave.
Phoenix, AZ 85006
The Art District's glassblowing studio.

Yayoi Kusama Firefly Infinity Mirror Room (installed permanently)
Phoenix Art Museum
1625 N. Central Ave.
Phoenix, AZ 85004

Monument Valley Navajo Tribal Park

Book a tour with company like Simpson's Trailhandler Tours

Located in Northern Arizona

Jeep tours are offered as well a 2 1/2 hour trek to some of the most photographed places in Monument Valley. You can also stay overnight in a tradition hogan.

Indian Reservations

Just as a heads up should you decide to visit any of the native American tribes, each of the tribes in Arizona is operated under its own government with rules for visitors, which are are different for each tribe. There is etiquette for touring tribal lands.

Be cautious when driving through reservations, especially at night as the land is usually open and the animals move about freely.

The reservation is home to those who live and work there and should be respected. Reservations are usually open to the public during the day. Private homes should only be entered by invitation only.

Many buildings are several hundred years old and should not be climbed, leaned or sit on. Nothing should be removed from the reservations including rocks, even pot shards.

Taking photos, audio, videos and even sketching is a very sensitive issue. Permission needed prior. Not complying can lead to confiscation of equipment or being asked to leave the reservation.

13

Best Restaurants

Here is a list of some of the best restaurants in Phoenix, Scottsdale and Old Scottsdale. You are sure to find something everyone will like on this list.

Mamma Toledo's The Pie Hole
15414 N. 7th St.
Phoenix, AZ 85022
Cuisine: Pie Shop $$

Fez
105 W. Portland St.
Phoenix, AZ 85003
Cuisine: Mediterranean / American $$

Oink Cafe
4326 E. Cactus Rd.
Phoenix, AZ 85032
Cuisine: Breakfast restaurant $$
Oink lives up to its name. A delicious breakfast and lunch spot

catering to the BACON lover. And there are several different ones to choose from.

Culinary Dropout
5632 N. 7th St.
Phoenix, AZ 85014
Cuisine: American $$

La Grande Orange Grocery
4410 N. 40th St.
Phoenix, AZ 85018
La Grande is a general store, wine shop, breakfast community spot and pizzeria all wrapped up in one. It has a Bohemian vibe and is open for breakfast, lunch and dinner. From breakfast to dessert...delish!

Fry Bread House
4545 N. 7th Ave.
Phoenix, AZ
Cuisine: Indian Fry Bread $
Most know that Arizona is home to many native Indians and one of our favorite native Indian foods is Frybread. This is a fried flat dough bread topped with honey, powdered sugar or jam, or various meats and other toppings. A frybread can be made like a taco with taco toppings. A must try!

Breakfast

Butterfield's Pancake House and Restaurant
7388 E. Shea Blvd.
Scottsdale, AZ 85260
Cuisine: Breakfast and Lunch $$

Snooze, an A.M. Eatery
2045 E. Camelback Rd.
Phoenix, AZ 85016
Cuisine: Breakfast $$

Snooze, an A.M. Eatery
15054 N. Scottsdale Rd.
Scottsdale, AZ 85254

Over Easy
4730 E. Indian School Rd.
Phoenix, AZ 85018
Cuisine: Breakfast $$

Matt's Big Breakfast
825 N. 1st St.
Phoenix, AZ 85004
Cuisine: Breakfast $$

Chinese / Japanese

China Chili
302 E. Flower St.
Phoenix, AZ 85012
Cuisine: Chinese $

Super Dragon
1212 E. Northern Ave.
Phoenix, AZ 85020
Cuisine: Chinese $

Kay Sushi
10115 E. Bell Rd.
Scottsdale, AZ 85260
Cuisine: Casual Japanese, Sushi

Kasai Scottsdale - Japanese Steakhouse
14344 N. Scottsdale Rd.
Scottsdale, AZ 85254
Cuisine: Japanese $$$

Ahipoki Bowl
1515 N. 7th Ave.
Phoenix, AZ 85003
Cuisine: Sushi $

Harumi Sushi and Sake
114 W. Adams St.
Phoenix, AZ 85003
Cuisine: Sushi $$

Dessert

Raspados Solaris
9204 N. 7th St.
Phoenix, AZ 85020
What is a raspados? It is generally a snow cone doused with a thick, delicious syrup and dressed with a bunch of fresh fruit and, depending on the one you order, ice cream too.

Frutilandia
Cuisine: Raspados (shaved ice dessert), Ice Cream, Fruit Desserts

Several locations in the Phoenix area - Phoenix, Tolleson, Glendale, Tempe, Mesa and Chandler

Churroholic

Cuisine: Churros (BIG ones), Ice Cream, Specialty Drinks and Coffees

Several locations in the Valley - Glendale, Peoria, Tempe, Tolleson (All within minutes of Phoenix)

Pie Snob

Several locations in the Phoenix and Chandler areas. They even have a pie vending machine with fresh pies.

The Sodamix

748 E. Bell Rd.

Phoenix, AZ 85022

Cuisine: Custom Sodas, Ice Cream and Cookies $

Churn

5223 N. Central Ave.

Phoenix, AZ 85012

Cuisine: Ice Cream $

Smallcakes Cave Creek

28255 N. Tatum Blvd

Cave Creek, AZ 85331

Cuisine: Cupcakes $$

Sweet Republic

Cuisine: Ice Cream, Confections $$

Several locations - Phoenix, Scottsdale and Tempe

Urban Cookies Bakeshop

2325 N. 7th St.

Phoenix, AZ 85006

Cuisine: Cookies, Cupcakes, Donuts and more

This bakeshop offers a variety of dairy free, vegan, nut free, soy free and gluten free options.

NY West Pastry and Bake Shop

10101 W. Grand Ave.

Sun City, AZ 85351

Here you can get native New York pastries and treats just a few minutes away instead of a few hours flight away.

Sicilian Baker

Several locations - Phoenix, Chandler and Peoria

Sicilian Baker has the largest variety of cannolis I have ever seen. They have a cannoli bar.

Mexican / Latin

Aunt Chiladas Squaw Peak

7330 N. Dreamy Draw Dr.

Phoenix, AZ 85020

Cuisine: Mexican $$

Aunt Chiladas (a little play on words) is a historic landmark that was built in the 1890s from railroad ties and desert stone. For some authentic Mexican food and some great cocktails, you must check out Aunt Chiladas.

Salvadoreno Restaurant - Pupusas

8911 N. Central Ave.

Phoenix, AZ 85020
Cuisine: Pupusas

What is a pupusa? It is a well known Salvadoran dish made from a thick corn tortilla stuffed with savory fillings of your choice like shrimp, cheese, refried beans, chicken, pork, etc.

Manuel's Mexican Restaurant and Cantina
1111 W. Bell Rd.
Phoenix, AZ 85023
Cuisine: Mexican $$

Mi Pueblo Mexican Food
710 E. Union Hills Dr.
Phoenix, AZ 85024
Cuisine: Mexican $

La Pinata
5521 N. 7th Ave.
Phoenix, AZ 85013
Cuisine: Sonora Style Mexican and Cocktails

La Pinata is said to be the home of the chimichanga. They are open from Tuesday to Sundays.

Pizza

Famous Ray's Pizza
350 E. Bell Rd
Phoenix, AZ 85022
Cuisine: Pizza $

Pizzeria Bianco

623 E. Adams St.
Phoenix, AZ 85004
Cuisine: Pizza $$
Several locations in the Phoenix area with slightly different names all listed on this website.

Pizza Heaven Bistro
5150 N. 7th St.
Phoenix, AZ 85014
Cuisine: Pizza $$

Gus' New York Pizza
2755 N. 91st Ave.
Phoenix, AZ 85037
Cuisine: Pizza $$

Thai

Authentic Thai Kitchen
4500 N. 12th St.
Phoenix, AZ
Cuisine: Thai $$

Thai Basil Signature Downtown Phoenix
114 W. Adams St.
PHoenix, AZ
Cuisine: Thai $$

Thai Recipe Bistro
2234 N. 7th St.
Phoenix, AZ 85006

Cuisine: Thai $$

Chanpen Thai - Phoenix
2727 E. Broadway Rd.
Phoenix, AZ 85040
Cuisine: Thai $

Vegan / Vegetarian / Gluten Free

Green New American Vegetarian
Nami
2014 N. 7th St.
Phoenix, AZ 85006

These two restaurants are next door to one another. Green is a delicious vegan restaurant. Nami is a vegan pastry, coffee and ice cream shop.

Loving Hut
3239 E. Indian School Rd.
Phoenix, AZ 85018

Verdura
5555 N. 7th St.
Phoenix, AZ 85014

Giving Tree Cafe
2024 N. 7th St.
Phoenix, AZ 85006

The Coronado
2245 N. 12th St.

Phoenix, AZ 85006

True Food Kitchen
2502 E. Camelback Rd.
Phoenix, AZ 85016

Flower Child
Several locations in the Phoenix area

Wildflower
Several locations in the Phoenix area

Plant Powered Kitchen
720 W. Highland Ave.
Phoenix, AZ 85013

Picazzo's Healthy Italian Kitchen Paradise Valley
Several locations in the Phoenix / Scottsdale areas

Old Town Scottsdale Restaurants

Culinary Dropout (Scottsdale Waterfront)
7135 E. Camelback Rd
Scottsdale, AZ 85251
Cuisine: American $$

The Mission
Old Town
3815 N. Brown Avenue
Scottsdale, AZ 85251
Cuisine: Latin $$$

The Mission
Kierland (Scottsdale)
7122 E. Greenway Pkwy
Scottsdale, AZ 85254

Bootleggers Modern American Smokehouse
7217 E. 1st Street
Scottsdale, AZ 85251
Cuisine: BBQ / Smoked $$

Bourbon & Bones
4200 N. Scottsdale Rd.
Scottsdale, AZ 85251
Cuisine: Steakhouse and bar $$$$

Olive & Ivy
7135 E. Camelback Rd.
Scottsdale, AZ 85251
Cuisine: American $$
Additional location at Phoenix Sky Harbor Airport
Cuisine: Mediterranean (Breakfast, Lunch and Dinner) $$

14

Hidden Gems - Restaurants

These are some of the hidden gems in Phoenix / Scottsdale area along with a few recommendations from a famous tv host.

Ziggy's Magic Pizza Shop

401 W. Van Buren St.
Phoenix, AZ 85003
Cuisine: Pizza $

Hanny's
40 N. 1st St.
Phoenix, AZ 85004
Cuisine: Bar $$
Hanny's features craft cocktails along with chic-casual cuisine in the downtown Phoenix area.

36 Below
3620 E. Indian School Rd.
Phoenix, AZ 85018
Cuisine: Cocktail Bar $$$
All I can say about 36 Below, please take a look at their website. There are no words to describe this gem.

Roy's Restaurant
5350 E. Marriott Dr.
Phoenix AZ 85054
Cuisine: Hawaiian fusion $$$
Roy's is located at the JW Marriott Hotel near Desert Ridge Mall. Beautiful setting. But nothing can touch their Hawaiian fusion cuisine.

Pop n Tea Bar
550 W. McDowell Rd.
Phoenix, AZ 85003
Cuisine: Dessert / Drinks $
Unique treats not found anywhere else. Menu of drinks built around teas and, of course, there is their specialties, popsicles. Their treats are

truly a work of art.

Mel's Diner

1747 Grand Ave.
Phoenix, AZ 85007
Cuisine: Diner $

Yes, we have a Mel's Diner from the 1970s iconic show with Alice, Mel, Vera and Flo.

Dick's Hideaway

6008 N. 16th St.
Phoenix, AZ 85016
Cuisine: Traditional Mexican $$

Serving breakfast, lunch and dinner, this is such a gem that it doesn't even display a sign on the outside of the restaurant. It is a rustic, yet casual upscale restaurant with a warm, low light feel. Nice and tucked away. A favorite for locals to bring their out-of-town guests for a special experience.

Match Market & Bar

1100 N. Central Ave.
Phoenix, AZ 85003
Cuisine: American $$

This upscale cafe and bar also has a market that is located in Downtown Phoenix in the Art District. The market features a variety of things from unique kitchen items to gourmet essentials to unique gift items from local sources.

Fuego at the Clarendon

401 W. Clarendon Ave.
Phoenix, AZ 85013

Cuisine: Latin Fusion $$

The Fuego features live music out on their patio every night. Nice relaxed setting. This is a storefront bar and bistro that serves mojitos, margaritas and Latin fusion fare.

The Arrogant Butcher
2 E. Jefferson St.
Phoenix, AZ 85004
Cuisine: American $$

The Arrogant Butcher has an awesome menu. From charcuterie boards to burgers and beer to ribs to crab legs AND more. Even their Happy Hour is impressive.

Diners, Drive-Ins and You Know What Features

Phoenix

Bootleggers
3375 E. Shea Blvd.
Phoenix, AZ 85028
Cuisine: American $$

Los Taquitos Mexican Grill
4747 E. Elliot Rd.
Phoenix, AZ 85044
Cuisine: Mexican $

Paradise Valley Burger Company
4001 E. Bell Rd.

Phoenix, AZ 85032
Cuisine: Burgers $$

Wild Thaiger
2631 N. Central Ave.
Phoenix, AZ 85004
Cuisine:

La Gourmet Taco Shop
1919 N. 16th St.
Phoenix, AZ 85006
Cuisine: Mexican $$
602-254-6330

Tacos Chiwas
1028 E. Indian School Rd.
Phoenix, AZ 85014
Cuisine: Mexican $

Over Easy
4730 E. Indian School Rd.
Phoenix, AZ 85018
Cuisine: Breakfast $$

Matt's Big Breakfast
825 N. 1st St.
Phoenix, AZ 85004
Cuisine: Breakfast $$

Giuseppe's on 28th
2824 E. Indian School Rd.

Phoenix, AZ 85016
Cuisine: Italian $$

Duce
525 S. Central Ave.
Phoenix, AZ 85004

Roberto's Mexican Food
39510 N. Daisy Mountain Dr.
Phoenix, AZ 85086

Barrio Cafe
2814 N. 16th St.
Phoenix, AZ 85006

St. Francis Restaurant
111 E. Camelback Rd.
Phoenix, AZ 85012

Scottsdale

Andreoli Italian Grocer
8880 E. Via Linda
Scottsdale, AZ 85258

Slanted Rice
6149 N. Scottsdale Rd.
Scottsdale, AZ 85250

Perk Eatery
6501 E. Greenway Pkwy

Scottsdale, AZ 85254

Toms' Thumb Market
9393 E. Bell Rd.
Scottsdale, AZ 85260

Defalco's Italian Grocery
2334 N. Scottsdale Rd.
Scottsdale, AZ 85257

15

Are We There Yet?

Here is an idea of how long it will take to get from point A to point B.

From Phoenix:

- Apache Junction - 45 minutes
- Grand Canyon - 3 ½ hours
- Camp Verde - 1 hour 20 minutes
- Sedona - 2 hours
- Jerome - 2 hours
- Prescott - 2 hours
- Flagstaff - 2 hours 20 minutes
- Prescott - almost 2 hours
- Rocky Point, Mexico - 4 hours
- Tucson - 2 hours
- Tombstone - 3 hours
- San Diego - 5 hours 45 minutes
- Los Angeles - 6 hours
- Las Vegas - 5 hours
- Holbrook - 3 hours

Phoenix Layout

Phoenix is split up like a grid. The main street down the middle is Central Avenue - running north to south. Every eight streets is a mile and is also a major street - running east to west. The 'avenues' are on the west side, while the 'streets' are on the east side. For example, 7th Avenue is west of Central avenue; while 7th Street is east of Central Avenue going toward Scottsdale.

Route 51 - Runs north / south from Loop 101 into the I-10.

Route 17 - Runs north / south from the end of the I-10 clear north. This is one of the roads to Arcosanti, Prescott, Jerome, Sedona, Flagstaff and the Grand Canyon and Las Vegas.

101 - Is one of 3 major loop highways (101, 202 and 303). Loop 101 takes you from west of Phoenix to Scottsdale to North Phoenix to Peoria to Sun City to the Peoria/Glendale area to Tolleson back to Phoenix.

I-10 - Runs east / west and can be taken from Phoenix through many of the suburbs like Tempe, Mesa, Tolleson, Goodyear, and Buckeye. It can be taken clear west to California and runs out east into Route 60.

Route 60 - Runs east / west through Tempe, Mesa, Gilbert out toward Apache Junction.

16

Conclusion

In closing, I hope this pocket guide was helpful in one way or another. This will be one of many gifts I will have for family and friends coming to visit or moving into the area. It's a nice introduction as to what one can find in the area...what one may not have even known they were looking for.

I plan on leaving a copy in my car as well for those leisure drives...even a gift to someone I may have just met that recently moved to the area. Then there's the friend who seems to be a bit of a homebody. You just never know when you need some help and a quick suggestion at your fingertips.

Safe travels and enjoy your time in the Valley of the Sun.

Just one last thought, Arizona has some of the most breathtaking sunrises and sunsets. I hope you get a moment to experience them while you are enjoying a cup of early morning java or a cocktail by the pool in the evening.

If you found this guide to be helpful, I would be very appreciative if you would leave a favorable review on Amazon. Thank you. :)

Amber Lea

Printed in Great Britain
by Amazon

27040136R00040